MW01290595

Warren Buffett Top Life Lessons

Warren Buffett Lessons for Unlimited Success in Business, Investing and Life

By Tatyana Williams

Published in Canada

© Copyright 2015 – Tatyana Williams

ISBN-13: 978-1507652800
ISBN-10: 1507652801

ALL RIGHTS RESERVED. No part of this publication may be reproduced or transmitted in any form whatsoever, electronic, or mechanical, including photocopying, recording, or by any informational storage or retrieval system without express written, dated and signed permission from the author.

Table of Contents

Introduction 1
  The Sage of Omaha 1

Chapter 1: Business 3
  1952-1962: Becoming a Millionaire in 10 Years 4
  1962-1990: The Path to Becoming a Billionaire 5
  1990-Today: The Richest Man in the World 7

Chapter 2: Investing 11
  Warren Buffett's Childhood Investments: Why Even Small
  Investment Can Lead to Great Wealth 11
  "I'm 15% Fisher and 85% Benjamin Graham": The Buffett
  Investing Strategy 13
  Taking the Right Risks 17

Chapter 3: Life 21
  Conviction and Commitment: Building Success from the
  Ground Up 21
  Materialism in Moderation: The Minimalist Lifestyle of
  Warren Buffett 23
  Surround Yourself with Success: Relationships are
  Investments 25

Conclusion 27
  Cultivating Success with Hard Work and Patience 27

Introduction

The Sage of Omaha

Warren Buffett has become a living legend because of his strong track record of sound investments and his overall success in everything he does. He is a prolific writer, publishing many books detailing the ways in which others could be as successful as he has become.

He was born on August 30, 1930 and by the young age of 32; he had already become a millionaire. A natural businessman, he began selling Coca Cola and chewing gum door to door as a child. He also took a job working at his grandfather's grocery store and filed for his first income tax return at just 14 years old. Warren Buffett purchased his first shares of stock at the age of 11 and would spend his free time as a child at the local stocker brokerage office.

After graduating with his Bachelors of Science in Business Administration at 19 years old, he went on to get his Masters of Science in Economics from the Columbia Business School where he studied under the tutelage of value investor Benjamin Graham.

Warren Buffett has become an inspiration for many and it is not uncommon to see investors structuring their portfolios to reflect the investments that he has made. However, his predilection for business and earning money does not come from greed or even a desire to be wealthy.

Despite being worth billions, Warren Buffett continues to lead a relatively modest lifestyle and gives large portions of wealth to charities and other philanthropic causes. A close friend to fellow business magnate, Bill Gates; Buffett intends to leave most of his wealth to the Bill and Melinda Gates Foundation after he dies.

The path to wealth was not always smooth for Warren Buffett. Anyone who studies his life and career closely will see that he has encountered obstacles, made mistakes and suffered loss just as any of us have. The difference between Warren Buffett and other people is not that he was born with a silver spoon in his mouth or that he was lucky enough to have a natural business savvy, it is that he does not let those losses or mistakes get in his way of success.

In fact, anyone can do what this man has accomplished if they follow his simple principles regarding business, investing and life. He has built his success on a strong foundation of hard work and perseverance; never giving up on his goals at any point in his life. By living your life with the same tenacity and ambition, you, too, can find success and fulfillment in life.

Chapter 1:
Business

Warren Buffett did not become wealthy because he was obsessed with money or with becoming the richest man alive. In fact, he plans to give the majority of his wealth to charity when he dies, leaving only a small sum for his children so that they will have a fair start in life. Buffett became wealthy because he is committed to the idea of working hard and dedicating yourself to what you want to achieve. His children will not inherit his billions because he intends for him to live by these same principles and build their own wealth and success.

1952-1962: Becoming a Millionaire in 10 Years

By the age of 20, Warren Buffett had managed to save $9,800 from his work and small business ventures throughout high school and college. Accounting for inflation, that $9,800 would amount to approximately $94,000 in today's dollars. That is $94,000 entirely from putting money away in savings.

After working for the family stock brokerage office in Omaha, Nebraska as an investment salesperson for three years, he took a job as a securities analyst at Benjamin Graham's partnership, earning a starting salary of $12,000 per year (or $105,000 in today's dollars).

By the time Graham closed his partnership and retired in 1956, Warren Buffett had built up a savings of $174,000 (approximately $1.4 million in today's dollars) with which he was able to start up his own investment partnership in his hometown of Omaha, Nebraska. To put that in perspective: his money had grown 17 times its original worth in just six years and he managed that purely by saving the money he had earned.

After starting his first partnership in 1956, Buffett began operating three separate partnerships within a year. By 1958, he was running five investment partnerships and by 1960 (when he was just 30 years old), that had grown to seven. Each of these partnerships was primarily built on the strategy of value investing.

Value investing means finding secure investments that are undervalued by the market and purchasing them at this "discounted" rate in order to earn a profit once the market corrects itself and the price of the stock grows to match its true or "intrinsic" value. This is typically regarded as a slow strategy with too low of a return to be useful for such remarkable gains as Warren Buffett saw.

However, by combining the principles of value investing instilled in him by Benjamin Graham and practicing more high risk investing as well, he was able to make all seven of his investment partnerships successful in just a couple short years. By 1962, the 32-year-old businessman had officially become a millionaire and merged all of his partnerships into one large investment company.

1962-1990: The Path to Becoming a Billionaire

After merging all seven partnerships into one large partnership worth more than $7 million (more than $1 million of which was directly owned by Buffett), he purchased a large amount of stock in Berkshire Hathaway, a struggling textile manufacturer, and eventually took over the business.

After making changes to the leadership of the company and restructuring the entire business by closing all of the mills and shifting it into the insurance sector, Berkshire Hathaway's stock (which his partnership originally began purchasing for $7.60 per share) was selling at $1,310 per share by 1979.

As he made multiple investments from 1962 to 1979—some through his investment partnership and some on his own—some fared better than others but his successes far outweighed his failures so that in less than two decades he had gone from being worth just over $1 million to having a net worth of an estimated $620 million in 1979. That represents a growth in his wealth of more than 600 times its original value.

Successes and failures persisted for Warren Buffett throughout the 1980s, including the purchase of a large stake in Coca Cola totaling about $1.02 billion in shares (or 7% of the company's total value) in 1988. This would end up being one of the most lucrative investments Buffett made through Berkshire Hathaway and the company continues to hold this investment in its portfolio even today.

Scandals arose regarding some of the investments made through Berkshire Hathaway throughout the years. In the mid-1970s, the SEC (Securities and Exchange Commission) investigated his company's acquisition of WESCO for possible conflicts of interest. There was concern that his parallel interests in Blue Chip, Berkshire Hathaway and Diversified Retailing manipulated the price of WESCO's stock in order to gain a majority holding in the company. After a thorough investigation, the SEC was unable to bring charges against Buffet himself; however, Blue Chip was charged with manipulation of stock prices and settled for $115,000.

In the mid-1980s, Buffett helped finance a merger of ABC and Capital Cities for $3.5 billion in return for a 25% controlling stake in the newly combined company. However, the merger was somewhat hampered by the need to comply with FCC rulings that forbid single companies from owning multiple media outlets in the same market. The company was forced to sell off some of its assets as a result.

On May 29, 1990, Berkshire Hathaway's stock (which he originally purchased for just $7.60 per share) closed at $7,175 per share; officially marking the moment when Warren Buffett became a billionaire.

1990-Today: The Richest Man in the World

After becoming a billionaire, Warren Buffett continued to do business and make investments, some of which ran into controversy particularly as the recession hit in 2007. In 2009, after accumulating personal wealth of more than $60 billion, Forbes declared him the richest man in the world, officially ending Bill Gates' 13-year reign of holding the title. Now the two business magnates (and friends) tend to alternate with each other for the title.

As an individual, Warren Buffett shifted heavily into philanthropic activities using his personal wealth to fund charities and other benevolent projects. In 2006, he announced that he would begin giving away 85% of his Berkshire holdings to various foundations in the form of annual gifts of stock. The largest portion of these gifts would go to the Bill and Melinda Gates foundation.

Warren Buffett, like millions of Americans, also suffered from the onset of the recession in 2007. Berkshire Hathaway suffered a heavy loss of 77% and several of his business deals suffered large losses. As the recession continued to hit the financial market heaviest, Buffett began to diversify Berkshire Hathaway's holdings by purchasing stock in other companies including 64 million shares in IBM.

This investment came as a surprise to many as Buffett had repeatedly claimed that he would never invest in technology because he did not fully understand it. However, he stated in an interview that the large purchase of stock was spurred by how high the company's corporate client retention rate was and his feeling that IBM had clearly defined goals and a concrete plan of how to achieve those goals.

This book will go into further details regarding Buffett's strategy for investing later on but for now, this purchase of IBM represents his tactic of looking at more than just the stock figures. For Warren Buffett, is equally important—if not more so—to look at the actual business itself and know what their business strategy is and whether or not it seems realistic or manageable.

From his current habits as a billionaire—namely his combination of strategic investments and large philanthropic donations—we can begin to get a sense of Warren Buffett's character. He is an ambitious businessman with a fondness for financial markets and investing but he is, by no means, greedy or extravagant. This is the key to his success. He is able to keep a sober and rational mind about his investments and wealth because he is not in business for the luxuries and riches but simply for the satisfaction he gets from his success.

Chapter 2:
Investing

Warren Buffett is worth nearly $60 billion and was ranked the richest man in the world in 2009 by Forbes. To be so wealthy, you would imagine he has a salary that is through the roof. In fact, he earns just $100,000 per year (less than some teachers). His wealth is generated entirely from his smart savings and investing tactics.

Warren Buffett's Childhood Investments: Why Even Small Investment Can Lead to Great Wealth

As mentioned in the introduction, Warren Buffett immersed himself in the goings on of the stock market since he was a small child. He made his very first purchase of stock at the age of 11 when he purchased three shares for himself and three shares for his sister in Cities Service, a gas and electric utilities company that later became Citgo.

At the age of 15, he and a friend invested $25 to purchase a pinball machine, which they placed in a local barbershop. The earnings they received from that pinball machine were used to buy more that they would place in different barbershops throughout town over the following months.

We can learn a lot from these early business ventures of Warren Buffett. He did not start out with millions in inherited wealth. Buffett relied entirely on his own earnings. The money he used to purchase stock in Cities Service came from his earnings from selling soda, chewing gum and magazines door to door in his neighborhood. The money to buy that first pinball machine came from his earnings from working in his grandfather's grocery store. The later pinball machines were purchased with the earnings he and his friend received from the first one.

It is often said that it takes money to make money. While this is true, we can see from Buffett's early years and steady ascension to becoming the richest man in the world that it does not take a lot of money to make money.

Spend your money well and you will not need to spend a lot. Even the smallest investments can give you high returns if you invest smartly and remain firm and consistent in your strategy.

So if you dream of one day investing, do not let a lack of wealth be your excuse for not starting. Simply do what you can to cut your expenses, living as frugally as you can reasonably manage while you save what you can each month as he did throughout his life.

You can really begin investing with any amount of money. Try to just save up $1,000 and invest it in a variety of stocks, which you can choose according to Warren Buffett's own investment strategy (discussed in detail in the next section). If you have the patience and perseverance to let your investments grow, you, too, can see the sort of success that Buffett has seen.

"I'm 15% Fisher and 85% Benjamin Graham": The Buffett Investing Strategy

To sum up Warren Buffett's investment strategy briefly, we would say that he follows the philosophy of value investing. Specifically, he applies Benjamin Graham's strategy of value investing in which he looks for stable, secure investments that are selling at lower rates than they should be according to their intrinsic or true worth. The basic principle here is that the market will eventually correct itself and the stock will begin selling at its true value once investors begin to see what the company is really worth.

This does not mean Buffett eliminates all risk and only buys stocks that are guaranteed to grow. There is no objective or concrete method for calculating a company's intrinsic worth. If there was, stocks would always be appropriately valued and this strategy would be useless.

Instead, value investors like Warren Buffett use individually selected criteria in order to estimate the true value of a given stock. That is, the value that the stock should actually be selling at. For Buffett—and here he differs from Graham and other value investors—the concern is not with the stock market. He does not invest in order to make gains in the financial market. Rather, he invests in order to have a percentage of ownership in strong companies that show an enduring ability to increase its profits consistently.

This means that Warren Buffett is not looking at the history of the company's stock or any of the ratios that many investors use to determine a stock's intrinsic value. He looks at the company as a whole, determining whether it has a strong business strategy and operates as close to optimal efficiency as possible.

When you begin to invest, then, do not concern yourself so much with how a given stock has done in the past. In fact, this is an all too common flaw in many investment strategies because past success does not guarantee future success. Many companies that dominated their market sector in the past have since fallen or collapsed entirely. Therefore, you are far better served by researching the company itself and finding out what its future plans are and how successful it could realistically be in achieving its goals.

Like Warren Buffett, choose investments as if you were choosing a company you want to own (because, in a sense, owning shares of a company's stock is akin to owning a percentage of that company). So is this a company you would feel confident in owning? If not, do not invest.

With that said, Warren Buffett uses a variety of criteria in order to determine whether a company has the potential to perform well.

A summary of the criteria Buffet uses when choosing which stocks to purchase include:

Return on Equity (ROE): Buffett looks at the company's records for the past 5 to 10 years to see how much the company earns per dollar invested (equity is essentially just another word for investments). If their ROE is consistently negative, you should probably avoid investing.

Debt to Equity Ratio (D/E ratio): He uses this figure to determine whether the company is taking on too much debt. Companies with high D/E ratios tend to be unstable because most of the growth in their revenue is coming from borrowed money that they will eventually need to pay back.

Profit Margins: Profit margins refer to the amount of money a company has earned after covering all of its fixed costs. That is, even if a company has earned $100 million in revenue from sales it becomes irrelevant if they spend $200 million just to operate. So profit margins show you not only how much they are earning but how efficiently they are operating. Buffett looks for companies with positive profit margins (i.e.-companies earning more than they spend) and, even further, for companies with profit margins that are growing year after year.

Longevity: This refers to how long a company has been around and, more importantly, how long it has been trading stock publically. For Warren Buffett, companies can only be considered as potential investments if they have been trading publically for at least 10 years.

Competitive Advantage: This is one of Warren Buffett's most unique criteria for valuing a company. It refers to how much a given company's product or service differs from its competitors. Buffett believes that companies who sell products that are too similar to its competitors can easily be overtaken by competing companies. Thus, the more unique and different a company's product is from its competitors, the more difficult it will be for those competitors to beat the company.

At least a 25% discount: In order to be considered a worthwhile value investment, Warren Buffett requires the current market value to be a minimum of 25% below his estimated intrinsic value.

The major key to success with this strategy, then, is accurately estimating a company's intrinsic value. This will take practice and perseverance because it is not something that you can objectively see in a company's financial records or historical progress. Therefore, it would be a good idea to practice Buffett's investing strategy before actually using it to invest real money.

Many stock simulation websites allow you to make hypothetical investments based on real market trends and see how successful your strategy would be in the real world. Use one of these to practice using his investment strategy while you are building up your savings in preparation for making actual investments. This way, you are better prepared and capable of making smarter investment decisions.

Taking the Right Risks

Smart investing—and smart living for that matter—is about taking the right risks. This has two components. First, do not make too risky of an investment or decision if it does not have a high enough payoff. Second, do not bet hesitant about taking risks if the reward is worth it. Achieving this balance is done by learning how to calculate risk and knowing when the odds are in your favor.

Before you can really know how to take risks, it is important to figure out what your risk tolerance is. That is, how much risk can you reasonably withstand? This depends on a variety of factors. After answering the four questions below, add up your points and find out what your risk tolerance is.

How many years do you have left until you retire?
    Less than 10 (1 point)
    Between 10 and 20 (2 points)
    20 years or more (3 points)

How much disposable income do you have each month? (i.e. - how much money do you have left over after covering all necessary expenses?)

    Less than 1,000 (1 point)
    Between $1,000-$10,000 (2 points)
    $10,000 or more (3 points)

What are (or would be) your primary goals as an investor?

    Building up a healthy retirement fund (1 point)
    Building up a healthy retirement fund and making some profit now (2 points)

Making as much profit now as possible (3 points)

What most closely resembles your typical attitude toward life?

I stay organized and keep everything on a tight schedule. I do not like surprises and I want to be sure I am prepared for every possible circumstance. (1 point)

I am fairly organized but I like to leave some room in my schedule so that I am free to follow my interests. I try to be prepared for everything but I know life can be unpredictable sometimes and I accept that. (2 points)

I rarely make set plans. I prefer to go with the flow and see where the current takes me. I solve problems on the spot as they come rather than worry about them beforehand. (3 points)

4-6 points: *low risk tolerance*. You have a low tolerance for risk. This might be because you only have a few years left to plan for retirement or because you do not have enough disposable income to be able to afford any heavy losses. Whatever the reason, you should be sure to stick with the safest possible investments and avoid taking chances on any high-risk investments.

7-9 points: *average risk tolerance*. This means you still have some time before you retire or you earn a decent income, allowing you to invest in some moderately risky assets. However, you should make sure your investment portfolio contains a balanced mixture of safe investments and riskier (but higher potential) ones.

10-12 points: *high-risk tolerance.* Either you have decades to go before you retire or you earn a substantial amount of money (or, perhaps, both). Whichever the case, you can afford to make some high-risk investments without suffering all that much. You may want to exercise a little caution just to make sure you have something to live on during your retirement years.

Chapter 3:
Life

Warren Buffett does not only apply his strategies and perspectives to business and investing. He also takes care to live his life according to those exact same principles. By being a dedicated and passionate businessman and balancing the ideals of moderation and generosity, Warren Buffett is able to live a gratifying life as both a successful entrepreneur and a satisfied husband and father. Work hard and follow these additional tips to be fulfilled at the innermost levels.

Conviction and Commitment: Building Success from the Ground Up

As you have probably noticed by now, one of the main things that sets Warren Buffett apart from others his lifetime of commitment to his goals. Since he was a young child, he has been interested in finance and building up successful businesses.

Because of this ambition, he dedicated his entire life to the pursuit of his goals. Spending his youth engaged in various small business ventures (such as purchasing a chain of pinball machines or selling products door to door) and saving up as much money as he could.

When he was just 17 years old, he began studying for his Bachelors in Business Administration, graduating at just 19 years old. He then went on to get his Masters in Economics and studied closely under Benjamin Graham who continues to be one of his greatest influences.

Even when Graham initially refused to hire Warren Buffett to his investment partnership, he never gave up. He took a job as an investment salesman back in his hometown and, just a few years later, Graham finally agreed to hire him.

Throughout his life, he was committed to building his savings eventually amassing $174,000 (or more than $1.4 million in today's dollars) just from money saved from his regular salary.

Therefore, in all things you hope to accomplish in your life, you should approach them with the same level of conviction and commitment that Warren Buffett has. The path to success is an upward climb and takes a lot of work, but if you commit to it and work tirelessly, you are sure to successfully make the climb.

Materialism in Moderation: The Minimalist Lifestyle of Warren Buffett

One of the most valuable lessons the man can teach us is how to live comfortably with our wealth but not extravagantly. As a successful billionaire, he could own mansions in every country, living beach side on some tropical island. However, he chooses to remain in this modest yet pleasant home in the Midwest.

Living frugally even when you can afford to live luxurious will not only help you to save money. It will also help you to realize what is truly important in life. The secret that Warren Buffett knows is that money truly *cannot* buy you happiness. It can buy you a sense of security and it can open many doors for you. However, happiness comes from being engaged in fulfilling work; from strengthening your relationships with those who are most important to you; from doing those things that make you happy.

Therefore, it does not matter whether you have a $30 million house or a $30,000 house. What matters are the people inside. This does not mean you should not enjoy the finer things in life. Even Buffett has a weakness for tailor-made suits.

Instead, only spend money on those things you actually enjoy. Do not buy a golf membership just because everyone else you know has one, unless you really enjoy golf. When you splurge, splurge on things that are actually be satisfying and only do it once you are sure all of your important expenses have been covered.

Even when you do find some luxury you enjoy spending money on, do not go overboard. Just like eating a meal: it is better to go slowly, savoring each bite rather than shoveling it down without taking the time to enjoy it. You may love high-end sports cars but that does not mean you should buy 15 of them.

Learn to cherish the things you do own and learn to enjoy yourself without spending a lot of money. One of Buffett's favorite activities is playing bridge with his friends and it does not cost a dime.

He began saving and investing at 11 years old because early on in life he understood the satisfaction of achieving long-term goals would be far greater than the instant gratification of caving into temporary urges. Learning to control your spending so that it is within your means is the key to living a satisfying, low stress lifestyle that can lead to better health and less debt.

Surround Yourself with Success: Relationships are Investments

One of the most important principles that Warren Buffett has stuck to is that of choosing whom you associate with carefully. He approaches his relationships as he does investments; asking whether or not this person will be an asset or a burden.

This does not mean putting a dollar value on your relationships but simply determining whether the person is lifting you up by providing encouragement or actual support. If someone is holding you back—perhaps by influencing you negatively or draining your energy and resources—they are like a bad investment that is consistently losing value.

Buffett chose to go to Columbia Business School because he knew that Benjamin Graham was there and that he could learn a lot from him. Like Buffett, you should seek out people who have a lot to teach you or who encourage and support you in your ambitions rather than weighing you down and holding you back.

Conclusion

Cultivating Success with Hard Work and Patience

Perhaps the most important lesson you can take from Warren Buffett is that, to be successful, you do not need to start out wealthy. Even the smallest investments can grow quickly in value if you are willing to put in the necessary effort to choose smart investments and work hard.

Another lesson we should take from the inspirational life of Warren Buffett is that of moderation. Working hard and putting as much money as possible into savings will help you to build up a healthy sum that you can eventually invest to grow your money even faster. Even if you put away just a small sum each month into a savings account, it will add up quickly and soon you can start building a healthy investment portfolio using the successful strategy that Warren Buffett uses himself.

If your goals are not necessarily to achieve financial success, cultivating Buffett's ambition and tireless commitment to working toward his goals will allow you to find the type of success you desire. So find out what you truly want in life, figure out the exact steps you will need to get there and then, start moving and refuse to give up no matter what obstacles life puts in your way.

ALL RIGHTS RESERVED. No part of this publication may be reproduced or transmitted in any form whatsoever, electronic, or mechanical, including photocopying, recording, or by any informational storage or retrieval system without express written, dated and signed permission from the author.

DISCLAIMER AND/OR LEGAL NOTICES:

Every effort has been made to accurately represent this book and it's potential. Results vary with every individual, and your results may or may not be different from those depicted. No promises, guarantees or warranties, whether stated or implied, have been made that you will produce any specific result from this book. Your efforts are individual and unique, and may vary from those shown. Your success depends on your efforts, background and motivation.

The material in this publication is provided for educational and informational purposes only and is not intended as medical advice. The information contained in this book should not be used to diagnose or treat any illness, metabolic disorder, disease or health problem. Always consult your physician or health care provider before beginning any nutrition or exercise program. Use of the programs, advice, and information contained in this book is at the sole choice and risk of the reader